Dedication

To my wise father and dear mother, Haddon and Bonnie Robinson,
who love me unconditionally and always encourage me.

And to my talented brother Torrey, with whom
I had to share a bathroom the entire time we were growing up.
Thank you for editing the copy and loving me. I love you. (Now.)

This book exists only because my friend,
author Brenda Smith, said, "I had the best idea. You should write for
Simple Truths! I can not tell you how strongly I feel about this!"

Brian Lord, Vice President at Premiere Speakers Bureau,
who has been both sales champion and loyal friend, helped make
that happen through a strong recommendation.

Brenda and Brian keep me feeling positive. I hope I tell them
often enough, "God blesses me through you."

Attitude
IS EVERYTHING

10 Rules for Staying Positive

VICKI HITZGES

Published by Simple Truths, 1952 McDowell Road,
Suite 205, Naperville, Illinois 60563

Simple Truths is a registered trademark.

Printed and bound in the United States
of America.

ISBN 978-1-60810-086-6

www.simpletruths.com
Toll Free 800-900-3427

Book Design: Vieceli Design Company,
West Dundee, Illinois

Editing by Stephanie Trannel

PHOTO CREDITS:
Cover image: Jim Rider : www.jimzrider.com
Images courtesy iStockphoto.com.

02 WOZ 10

Table of Contents

Introduction

I used to wonder how they did it. How could positive people stay so upbeat? You know the ones I'm referring to: They brighten rooms just by walking in. No matter what trials may be going on in their lives, they give you the same hospitality you expect to receive while visiting Orlando. Everybody wants to be around them.

We prefer positive people because it's no fun spending time with a person as chilly as an igloo. We enjoy warm, cheerful, upbeat folks who believe in us and remind us that tomorrow is ripe with possibility.

Most of us want to be positive people. It's advantageous to possess a sunny outlook. Doors open to optimists. They make friends, earn respect, close sales, produce loyal clients, and others enjoy and want to be like them. The question is how can we do that? What does it take to be positive? How can we grin instead of grouch?

Good news! If you want to pep up
your outlook, this book tells how.
Never forget... Attitudes are contagious.
Always ask... Is mine worth catching?
I hope it will be!

~ **Vicki Hitzges** ~

RULE # 1

WAIT TO WORRY

I used to worry. A lot. The more I fretted, the more proficient I became at it. Anxiety begets anxiety. I even worried that I worried too much! Ulcers might develop. My health could fail. My finances could be depleted to pay the hospital bills.

A comedian once said, ***"I tried to drown my worries with gin, but my worries are equipped with flotation devices."*** While not a drinker, I certainly could identify! My worries could swim, jump and pole vault!

To get some perspective, I visited a well known, Dallas business-man, Fred Smith. Fred mentored such luminaries as motivational whiz Zig Ziglar, business guru Ken Blanchard and leadership expert John Maxwell. Fred listened as I poured out my concerns and then said,

"Vicki, you need to learn to wait to worry."

As the words sank in, I asked Fred if he ever spent time fretting. (I was quite certain he wouldn't admit it if he did. He was pretty full of testosterone—even at age 90.) To my surprise, he confessed that in years gone by he had been a top-notch worrier!

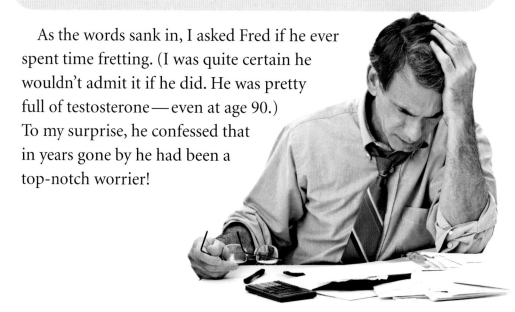

> *"Anxiety does not empty tomorrow of its sorrow, but only empties today of its strength."*
>
> — **CHARLES SPURGEON,** *English Preacher*

As a young man, Fred landed a high-paying executive job. Yet he'd only earned a high school degree. He was afraid someone with a college degree would come along and snag his job. Each night after work, he sat with a cup of coffee worrying about losing his position because he thought no other job could compare to the one he had. (In light of his subsequent successes, he chuckled to recall that particular fear.) **As he fretted, he started to realize that he wasn't anxious based on fact, he was anxious based on his imagination. He was borrowing trouble.**

He thought to himself, "Fred, are you a better, more valuable employee if you stay up late worrying? Do you do your best work if you're tired and tense?

WHAT WERE YOU WORRYING ABOUT THIS TIME LAST YEAR?

"I decided that I would wait to worry!" he explained. **"I decided that I'd wait until I actually had a reason to worry—something that was happening, not just something that might happen—before I worried.** As it turns out, I never lost that job. My boss was very happy with my performance."

"When I'm tempted to get alarmed," he confided, "I tell myself, 'Fred, you've got to wait to worry! Until you know differently, don't worry.' And I don't. Waiting to worry helps me develop the habit of not worrying and that helps me not be tempted to worry."

Fred possessed a quick mind and a gift for gab. As such, he became a captivating public speaker. "I frequently ask audiences what they were worried about this time last year. I get a lot of laughs," he said, "because most people can't remember. Then I ask if they have a current worry—you see nods from everybody. Then I remind them that **the average worrier is 92% inefficient—only eight% of what we worry about ever comes true."**

My friend Sally Lain agrees with Fred. Sally waits to worry. Sally loves to get up each morning and rejoice.

Many people fail to rejoice today because they live with the worry of tomorrow's threats, evil and sorrow. Something fearful might happen and they can't ignore it. If we worry about something that has not occurred, theologian Helmut Thielicke calls it, "wandering in times not our own."

> *"If pleasures are greatest in anticipation, just remember that this is also true of trouble."*
>
> — **ELBERT HUBBARD,** *American Writer*

The great preacher, Dr. Haddon Robinson, points out, **"People seldom, if ever, are destroyed by what happens on one particular day. What really does us in is our worry about what might happen tomorrow... And when we think of it, no**

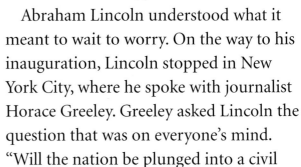

crisis has ever happened in the future."

Abraham Lincoln understood what it meant to wait to worry. On the way to his inauguration, Lincoln stopped in New York City, where he spoke with journalist Horace Greeley. Greeley asked Lincoln the question that was on everyone's mind.

"Will the nation be plunged into a civil war?" Lincoln responded to Greeley's question with an anecdote about some lawyers from Illinois. They followed the judge from town to town to argue cases. As they traveled, they had to cross a number of rivers, including many that were swollen. They were particularly worried about the Fox River. In a small town where they had stopped for the night, they met a circuit-riding preacher.

He had crossed the Fox River many times, so they asked him about it. "I have one rule that helps me cross the Fox River," he said. "I don't cross the Fox River until I get there."

Are you worried? Don't cross the river until you get there. Take Fred's advice: **Wait!**

By the way, you can enjoy Fred Smith's insights—free!
Visit www.BreakfastWithFred.com
Pssst—While you're there, sign up for the Weekly Thought.

"How simple it is to see that all the worry in the world cannot control the future. How simple it is to see that <u>we can only be happy now</u>. And that there will never be a time when it is not now."

— GERALD JAMPOLSKY, *Physician*

RULE # 2

Keep an ATTITUDE *of*
GRATITUDE

Years ago, I was the public relations director for motivational guru, Zig Ziglar. At the time, he was arguably the best-known, most loved speaker in the world. When audience members heard Zig, they witnessed a man chockfull of energy, vitality and joy. Having worked closely with him and knowing him well, I can tell you that the Zig you saw on stage was the real Zig Ziglar. In fact, I can't remember ever seeing him when he was not happy and upbeat.

The Zig I knew was one carbonated guy.

Every time Zig answered his home phone, he picked up the receiver and said with gusto, "This is Jean Ziglar's happy husband!" And he meant it!

Awhile back one of Zig's closest friends and I were discussing Zig's aura of happiness. "Completely genuine," his friend said. **"I have never seen him down."** Then he added thoughtfully, but with love, "Hardly what you'd call normal."

Mrs. Ziglar's Gratitude Recipe:

WORK, LOVE, FAITH

"What's Zig's secret?" I asked.

"I think," he said, "it comes down to feeling grateful. Never met a guy more grateful than Zig. Period."

You'd think anyone that grateful must have had an easy life. But that's not so.

Zig started out poor. Dirt poor. His father died when he was six, leaving his mother to raise 11 children alone. The family was virtually

Remember what Mom said...
Always say "please" and "thank you."

penniless. Yet despite their poverty, Mrs. Ziglar instilled a strong work ethic in her children and raised them to believe that both she and God loved them. She also instructed her children to practice saying "please" and "thank you." Those lessons stuck. Her formula of work, love and faith made their difficult lives easier. Gratitude made their lives enjoyable.

Zig once told me, "When we neglect to require our children to say 'thank you' when someone gives them a gift or does something for them, we raise ungrateful children who are highly unlikely to be content. **Without gratitude, happiness is rare. With gratitude, the odds for happiness go up dramatically.**"

Zig and his wife, Jean, "the Redhead" (the pet name he gave her), had four children — Suzan, Cindy, Julie and Tom. Suzan, the oldest, not only inherited her mother's looks and vivacious smile, she also inherited a passion from both her parents to encourage others.

HAVE AN ATTITUDE OF GRATITUDE.

One day Suzan fell ill. Within a short time, she was fighting for her life. The doctors prescribed steroids that made her bloated, large and uncomfortable. In a matter of just a few months, the unthinkable happened—Suzan died. Jean and Zig were heartbroken.

At the viewing at the funeral home, I was struck by how upbeat Zig appeared. Despite his grief, he was his usual self: He smiled and shook hands with friends and offered comfort to others who grieved. His strong Christian faith gave him hope that he'd see Suzan again. But there was something else: "We have no regrets," Zig told several well-wishers. **"She knew we loved her. We feel no regret." Even in his deepest sorrow, Zig counted his blessings and that buoyed his sagging spirits.**

Years ago, Zig created the popular phrase, "Have an attitude of gratitude." According to Zig, "The more you recognize and express gratitude for the things you have, the more things you will have to express gratitude for."

I know firsthand that giving thanks brings joy. Awhile back, I heard Oprah Winfrey urge viewers to keep a Gratitude Journal. It seemed pretty schmaltzy to me, so I didn't do it. But Oprah was a jackhammer. Day after day, week after week, she kept pounding on that idea. I'd catch her show here and there. Same thing: Keep a Gratitude Journal. A few months later, I was speaking to a government group and staying in a cruddy hotel. I was seated at the hotel's indoor restaurant by a swimming pool reeking with enough chlorine to purify the Love Canal. As I waited impatiently for my

> *"It's not easy being grateful all the time. But it's when you feel least thankful that you are most in need of what gratitude can give you."*
>
> **—OPRAH WINFREY,**
> *TV Talk Show Host, Actress, Editor and Producer*

> "Gratitude unlocks the fullness of life.
> It turns what we have into enough, and more.
> It turns denial into acceptance, chaos to order,
> confusion to clarity. It can turn a meal into a feast,
> a house into a home, a stranger into a friend.
> Gratitude makes sense of our past, brings peace
> for today, and creates a vision for tomorrow."
>
> — **MELODY BEATTIE**, *Therapist, Author*

meal to arrive, I suddenly remembered Oprah's directive. What the heck? I had a pen and some scrap paper.

I listed my mother who spent time each day praying for me. I wrote down my father who deeply loves me. My kind, funny brother and his family. My job and the opportunity to travel and encourage people. Friends. Laughter. For the fact that I had a place to sleep that was safe. For a private bathroom. (You start listing— you begin to get thankful!) **I quickly listed about 30 things and noticed that not only did I have a lot to be thankful for, but suddenly I was in a terrific mood!**

Publisher Malcolm Margolin was grateful for something that's right outside our doors, but most of us have never taken the time to experience it. He wrote,

"The next time it begins to rain... lie down on your belly, nestle your chin into the grass and get a frog's-eye view of how raindrops fall... The sight of hundreds of blades of grass bowing down and popping back up like piano keys strikes me as one of the merriest sights in the world."

That might strike you as advice from a person with not nearly enough to do, but personally, I like it. If Margolin can feel joy in soggy clothes looking at wet grass, you and I can find all kinds of things for which we can give thanks!

Count your blessings. Jot them down.

At least stop and think of as many things as you can that you're thankful for right now. It worked for Oprah, Zig, Margolin and me. Give it a shot. If you want to feel happy, try on an attitude of gratitude for a change in your mood, your outlook and you.

"*Feeling gratitude and not expressing it is like wrapping a present and not giving it.*"

— WILLIAM ARTHUR WARD

RULE # 3

YOUR HEALTH

is Your WEALTH

M y Grandpa Robinson used to say, "Vicki, if you have your health, you have everything." As a kid, I thought he was nuts. I had my health but I didn't have a Barbie Dream House. So much for his "everything" theory! Now that I'm older, I realize that what he said was an overstatement, but the reverse of what he said had truth glued all over it. ***If you lose your health, you lose everything.***

It doesn't matter how rich you are. It doesn't even matter if you have a Barbie Dream House (or a mansion, a yacht or a new Rolls Royce). If your health fails and you feel lousy, you're not going to enjoy it.

Your health is your wealth. So, what can you do to protect this important asset? Get in shape! It's one of the most positive moves you can make. Why?

Because getting fit gives you energy, increases your endurance and builds your confidence.

When you exercise or lift weights, your body releases endorphins. Endorphins have been linked to the same kind of high produced by morphine! (And they're legal!) When you are pumped full of endorphins, you look better, think better, feel better and sleep better.

30 minutes
of intense aerobic exercise immediately reduces body tension.

We've all heard it's not good to ***"sweat the small stuff,"*** but sometimes it can be fantastic to just sweat!

A study done at California State University showed that 30 minutes of intense aerobic exercise immediately reduces body tension. **Research at Hofstra University in New York City showed that weight lifting stops anxiety and boosts self-esteem as well as, if not better than, aerobic exercise.** Do both! You'll look and feel terrific…plus, the stress relief will help you sleep like a fraternity pledge in an 8 a.m. class.

Speaking of sleep, get some! Get lots.

Your body heals and repairs itself while you sleep. Most Americans don't get enough. According to *The National Sleep Foundation*, adults need between seven and nine hours of sleep every night. If you have trouble getting enough rest, here are some suggestions:

Stick to a schedule.
Go to bed at the same time every night, even on weekends.

Create a bedtime routine.
You could try soaking in a warm tub and then listening to relaxing music or reading an interesting book. Do the same thing every night. Start about an hour before you plan to turn out the lights.

Make your bedroom dark, quiet and cool. If you keep even a small light glowing, your body might not produce melatonin which helps you sleep.

"To be or not to be isn't the question. The question is *how* to prolong being."

— **TOM ROBBINS**,
American Author

7 to 9

HOURS PER NIGHT

No liquids two hours before bedtime. **You want to sleep, not shuttle back and forth from your bed to your bathroom.**

Avoid coffee, tea, soft drinks and alcohol. **For most people, caffeine shakes things up like a loose dog at a cat show. Alcohol, on the other hand, lulls you to sleep then wakes you up later.**

Cold feet? Wear socks. **Cold feet are like dull library books: They have poor circulation. Keep them warm or they'll keep you up.**

> "Eating everything you want is not that much fun. When you live a life with no boundaries, there's less joy. If you can eat anything you want to, what's the fun in eating anything you want to?"
>
> — **TOM HANKS**, *Actor*

In addition to exercise and sleep, watch your diet.

Generally, blow off everything "white"—white flour, white sugar and starchy potatoes. Load up on fresh vegetables with deep, rich colors. In fact, the deeper the color the better.

Steam broccoli and asparagus, slurp pomegranate juice, pop blueberries and roast tomatoes in olive oil for super healthy, nutrition-packed treats. If you haven't tried it, peel and freeze a banana for a tasty snack on a hot summer day. Or chomp on frozen grapes for a healthy, fun treat!

Someone once asked the great actress Katharine Hepburn what it takes to be successful. She answered,

"One of the main qualities it takes to be successful is energy." Then she paused and added, "Energy may be the only thing!"

That may be a very simplistic formula for success, but winning in life has a lot to do with having the energy you need to accomplish what you want in life.

You may think that you don't have time to exercise 30 minutes a day or to sleep eight hours a night or even to eat right. The reality is that if you don't make time to take care of yourself, you'll be forced to find time to be sick. Make time!

Realize that your health is your wealth.
Want it to grow? Make yourself a priority.
You're worth it!

"It is health that is real wealth and not pieces of gold and silver."

— MAHATMA GANDHI

RULE # 4

The SERIOUS BENEFITS *of*
BELLY LAUGHS

Knock knock?

Who's there?

When I was a kid, my favorite time of day was dinner. It wasn't for the food (my mother cooked liver!). It was because my parents, my brother and I sat at the table and laughed together. We would linger over dinner long after the meal was gone, talking and teasing each other with great affection. I especially liked it when I could make my brother laugh hard enough to snort milk through his nose.

Now we know that laughter doesn't just make life fun, it keeps us healthy, releases endorphins and it can even cure diseases! Now that's worth having liquid shoot out your nose!

PEOPLE WITH HEART DISEASE WERE **40%** LESS LIKELY TO LAUGH IN HUMOROUS SITUATIONS THAN THOSE WITH HEALTHY HEARTS.

One of the most famous laughers of all times is Norman Cousins. Cousins was a magazine editor who got a bad diagnosis in 1964. Doctors found that the connective tissue in his spine was deteriorating. **One of those doctors, a close friend, told him that his chance of survival was approximately 1 in 500.** (Nothing to laugh about there!) Realizing that death was a very real probability, Cousins took action. He took three radical steps against his doctors' advice.

First, he researched all the various drugs he was taking. He discovered that his condition depleted his body of Vitamin C. Based primarily on Cousins' personal research, his doctors agreed to inject him with mega-doses of the supplement.

Second, Cousins checked himself out of the hospital and into a hotel. Because Cousins believed hospitals had haphazard hygiene practices, a culture of overmedication, feelings of negativity and routines that kept patients from sleeping, he felt hospitals were "no place for a person who is seriously ill."

Third, Cousins grabbed a movie projector, an armload of Marx Brothers' movies and a bunch of *Candid Camera* episodes. He set up a projector in his hotel room and laughed so hard watching the funny clips that his stomach hurt.

"Laughter is the   shock absorber

His laughter stimulated enough natural chemicals to allow him to sleep peacefully for several hours. When pain woke him back up, he would switch the projector back on again until he laughed himself back to sleep.

Cousins reasoned that if negative emotions like anger and resentment could make someone sick, positive emotions like happiness and laughter could make someone well! He knew he was on the right track because he measured the changes in his body as he laughed by measuring the blood sedimentation rate, a key measure of inflammation and infection in the blood. His rate dropped by at least five points each time he watched a funny show.

that eases the blows of life."

Instead of taking massive doses of drugs and feeling fear, Cousins literally laughed himself back to health! Within a few weeks, he was back at work at the *Saturday Evening Review*. Apparently, his positive emotion theory proved correct.

Even if Cousins' cure was a one-time fluke, all kinds of other experiments show that laughter will keep you alive and smiling!

The Associated Press ran an article that claimed laughter may be good for the heart. A team of Maryland medical researchers at the Center for Preventative Cardiology at the University of Maryland Medical Center found that people with heart disease were 40 percent less likely to laugh in humorous situations than those with

> ## "What soap is to the body, laughter is to the soul."
>
> **— YIDDISH PROVERB**

healthy hearts. It is uncertain, however, whether humor helps prevent heart problems or if people with heart problems tend to lose their sense of humor.

Dr. Rose Marie Robertson, a Vanderbilt University cardiologist said a study of 300 people, half of whom had histories of heart problems, used questionnaires to gauge how healthy people and those with heart disease differed in their responses to situations where humor was expected. The people with heart disease were much less likely to even recognize humor. They also laughed less even in positive situations and generally displayed more anger and hostility than people with healthy hearts. **(Lesson: If you're uptight—loosen up! Not only will you get more party invitations, you'll live a long time and enjoy going!)**

Need a good cleanse on the inside?

Find a funny friend.

Have dinner with someone who
makes you laugh out loud. See a
movie that makes you laugh
'til you cry. You need a bath!
On the inside.

"A sense of humor...
is needed armor. Joy in one's heart
and some laughter on one's lips
is a sign that the person down deep
has a pretty good grasp of life."

— **HUGH SIDEY**

RULE # 5

JOY BOOMERANGS

You know how when you do some-thing nice for someone—bring an unexpected gift to a friend, compliment a waitress, return a windblown hat to a stranger—it makes you feel better? If you do that repeatedly, it could help you in all kinds of ways. In fact, if you become altruistic and put others first, research indicates that you will probably die smiling. Fortunately, you'll be happy, so you won't mind.

Obviously that's an exaggeration (you probably will mind), but do good for others, and you'll be surprised at how helping them will help you.

For example, in the mood to share? Go ahead! It will make you happy. Stephen Post, Director of the Center for Medical Humanities, Compassionate Care and Bioethics at Stony Brook University in New York, says,

> *"Happiness is a byproduct of living generously."*

The *Journal Science* published a study that examined the relationship between philanthropy and well-being. Researchers analyzed the spending patterns of more than 600 men and women, then questioned them about their general happiness. When subjects spent money to pay bills or buy items for themselves, they didn't report feeling happier. Yet when subjects spent money buying gifts or donating to charities, their actions made them feel much happier. The bottom line? You don't get happiness. It comes from what you give.

Think you look fat in those pants? Volunteer! No kidding. Get this! According to the *The Journal of Gerontology: Social Sciences*,

RESEARCH FINDING

African-American women aged 60 and older who volunteered in elementary schools burned twice as many calories as those who did not!

How cool is that?! Help out in a school and get thin thighs! Where do we sign up?

Dr. Erwin Tan from Johns Hopkins University says that working with children may be as good for the volunteers' health as getting a gym membership. *In addition, because the volunteers enjoy working with children, they may be more willing to stick with the activity compared to a traditional exercise program.* The kids get love and care, the adults get joy and a good workout! That's a win-win!

By the way, the research focused on African-American women because the study took place in two communities where black women tended to volunteer. The results likely would be the same for all seniors.

What's more, the study showed that increased physical activity from volunteering usually remains high for at least three years! Now that's a payoff!

In the December 2008 issue of *The Gerontologist*, you'll find another encouraging study about volunteers. Michelle Carlson, Ph.D., led a research team at Johns Hopkins University that found volunteers showed greater improvements in memory and executive function than those who did not participate. In fact, older adults most at risk for health disparities and who donated their time, showed the most significant gains.

IF YOU VOLUNTEER, YOU'LL NOT ONLY FEEL BETTER, BURN CALORIES AND SHARPEN YOUR MIND, BUT YOU ALSO HAVE A GREATER CHANCE OF LIVING LONGER!

> *"I don't know what your destiny will be, but one thing I know: the only ones among you who will be really happy are those who have sought and found how to serve."*
>
> — **ALBERT SCHWEITZER,** *Humanitarian and Physician*

Researchers at the University of Michigan surveyed 1,211 adults over 65 (mostly retirees), then checked up on them eight years later. The subjects who volunteered at least 40 hours each year to a single cause were 40 percent more likely than non-volunteers to be alive at the end of the study. The findings took into account differences in the two groups' incomes, health and the number of weekly social interactions. Interestingly, the most important factor seemed to revolve around volunteering at just one spot.

Volunteers who spread their time among several organizations did not gain an advantage in longevity.

THE BOTTOM LINE IS THIS:

Do unto others as you'd like to have done unto you. Apparently the good you do boomerangs and comes back to you!

For a happy, healthy, positive life, share your money and yourself.

"If you want to lift yourself up, lift up someone else."

— BOOKER T. WASHINGTON

RULE # 6

LOSING *the* FIGHT?

WRITE

S tudies have shown that about 30 percent of women are reportedly depressed. (That 30 percent is probably the area from their bust to their thighs!) The depression rate among males was originally estimated to be about half that, but more recent studies show that it's higher.

No matter where you fall in the depression line-up, male or female, giddy or groaning, at one time or another you can bet you'll spend some time feeling down. **When you feel that you're losing the fight, start to write!**

How?

1 *Journal*

One of the best things you can do when you find yourself in the valley is to write about what you're feeling. Note what's happening to you and what effect your circumstances have on your emotions. Whatever comes into your mind, scribble it down.

Don't edit your thoughts, just capture them.

Whether you scribble your feelings on paper or clack your thoughts into a computer, journaling lets you release frustrations, hurts and confusing emotions. Like letting a shaken can of Coke spew open, journaling releases pent-up feelings, leaving you more relaxed and calm. As a result, you'll find yourself better able to move forward.

If you journal your feelings you'll benefit both mentally and physically. Get this: James Pennebaker, Ph.D., professor of psychology at the University of Texas at Austin, the author of *Opening Up: The Healing Power of Expressing Emotions*, found that writing about upsetting experiences for just 20 minutes at a time, over three or four days, can boost your immune system and make your blood pressure drop significantly. *Get out your pen and say, "Ahhh."*

> *"You must stay drunk on writing so reality cannot destroy you."*
>
> — **RAY BRADBURY,** *American Writer*

2 Set Goals

If you feel "stuck" after you write down your thoughts, spend time setting goals. You'll probably find that journaling your emotions will calm you, while writing goals will energize you. Many people enjoy journaling to get rid of their negative feelings and then setting goals to focus on a bright future. **By putting your goals in writing, you move from victim to victor.**

Seeing your goals in black and white will boost your spirits.

You really can change your life! Have you ever had the dream where you're naked? Or the one where you're about to take the final exam and you haven't gone to class all semester? Or the dream where you're about to take the final exam, you haven't gone to class all semester *and* you're naked? According to research reported in Men's Health magazine, you can banish your bad dream, or any other nightmare, simply by reworking it. In the study, 39 people who had recurring nightmares agreed to think about their nightmare and change its plot, write down a new dream and mentally rehearse it. The result? Their bad dreams decreased dramatically. In essence, they set a goal for dreaming!

So think about this: *How do you want your life to turn out? If you don't like the plot your life is taking, rework it! Take out a piece of paper and re-fashion. Set goals, break big goals into day-to-day manageable chunks, set deadlines, mentally rehearse your success by visualizing it and then start!*

3 Send a Note

Thank you for being there for me!

Send a note to encourage someone else. Keep note cards and pre-stamped postcards handy so you can easily jot a letter to someone who needs a boost. You can't make someone else happy without making yourself happy.

Bonnie Robinson has friends all over the world. Literally. She meets people in the grocery story, at church, at recitals, at the movies, almost everywhere she goes. Wherever she meets people, if they need encouragement, she gets their address. Then, depending on the situation, she drops them either a sympathetic note or a cheery card. Students living overseas, physicians, attorneys, mothers, accountants, designers, musicians…all sorts of people testify they've had their spirits lifted when they opened their mailbox and found a handwritten note from her. In this high-tech world, a hand-written, stamped letter is a little gift!

> *"If I don't write to empty my mind, I go mad."*
> — **LORD BYRON**, *Romantic Poet*

It's always heartening to know someone cares. What's more, Bonnie feels good knowing she makes other people feel good.

Feeling down or lost? Grab a pen and some paper and pull back onto the road to happiness. **Journal.**

Write down your goals. Send someone a note letting them know that you care. It will surprise you how much better you'll feel quickly.

"*If my doctor told me I had only* **six minutes to live,** *I wouldn't brood. I'd type a little faster.*"

— **ISAAC ASIMOV**, *American Author and Scientist*

RULE # 7

KEEP THE FAITH, BABY

It seems unbelievable to me now, but when I first met Thelma Wells, I didn't like her. She just seemed too good to be true. Thelma's a successful speaker. She's funny. She's always laughing and saying "religious" things. The more she talked, the phonier she seemed. I couldn't relate to a nonstop happy-faced, religious person who cracked jokes, shook her hands in the air and turned problems into comedy routines.

When we met, I was slogging through a painful divorce. "Thelma," I thought, "you go through some pain and then talk to me about joy." **Heartache never visited Thelma. She didn't know how it hurts to not feel loved.** Every time I saw Thelma, she seemed happy, happy, happy. Thelma didn't understand real life. Everything always went well for her. Or so I thought.

One day Thelma and I both spoke at the same meeting and, for the first time, I heard Thelma's life story. As I listened, my love for her took root.

Thelma's teenaged parents never married. Thelma never knew how it felt to have a mother smother her with kisses, read to her or tell her that she loved her. "My mother was a cripple," Thelma says, "She couldn't raise me. I only vaguely remember ever seeing my father. He stopped by a few times. Then his visits ended completely." Thelma never knew her father's family.

Thelma's mother's father lived in a tiny room and worked, so he couldn't raise her. But he loved Thelma, so he asked his parents to raise her. Thelma's great-grandparents agreed, but

"True spirituality does not
make me significant,
but peaceful and joyful."

—**FRED SMITH,** *Businessman/Mentor*

Thelma's great-grandmother resented her and treated her cruelly.

In the mornings after her husband left for the day, **Thelma's great-grandmother would force Thelma into a dark closet.** Thelma stayed locked up until right before her great-grandfather returned at night.

If you have children or remember your fears as a child, you know how scared children feel in the dark. Add to that an evil, old woman, no escape, threats and loneliness.

Amazingly, Thelma survived.

"Every Sunday my great-grandfather took me to church where I learned hymns. I loved music," she says, "and the only

music I knew came from church. While I was in the closet, I didn't have anything to do," she recalls, "so I just sang."

"I don't ever remember feeling angry or scared," she told me recently. "When I was locked up, I sang hymns until I fell asleep. See, I didn't know it then, but I was worshiping. And do you know, I don't ever remember feeling angry at my great-grandmother?! In fact, I didn't realize until I was in my 30s that what she did to me was child abuse! **When I sang those hymns, I felt happy and the words from those songs helped build my faith!"**

If you want to feel happy and positive, don't shortchange religious faith. In the secular book, *Gross National Happiness*, author Arthur Brooks found that people with more faith and religion in their lives feel happier than those who have little or none.

Thelma's story bears that out. "I had to care for my great-grandmother when she got old," Thelma recalls. "She hated me until her dying day. She never thanked me and she said mean things to the very end. But because of my faith, I was able to show love to her. I can honestly say that while I cared for her, I felt joy."

1/3

People with faith are one-third less likely to die in a given period than those who don't have faith.

Wow. But there's more: Not only can religious belief brighten our outlook, research also shows a link between faith and longevity. People with faith are one-third less likely to die in a given period than those who don't. In fact, Dan Buettner from the National Institute of Aging, wrote in his book, *The Blue Zones*, that even people who are not church-goers, but who do have spiritual beliefs have less depression, better immunity and less heart disease than those who have no spiritual beliefs.

As a child, Thelma believed the hymns she sang assured her she was loved and not alone. She finds assurance in that belief today.

It's difficult for people to go through life without faith. After all, if you believe that everything in life depends on you, that works when things go well and you enjoy health and success. But how do you stay positive when your health fails, your job goes away, your children rebel or your marriage crumbles? If we believe that we are left to ourselves, we are left alone and we are frail. On the other hand, if we have someone else upon whom we can depend to guide our destiny, who loves and cares for us, we will feel much more positive.

Thelma's life, I've since learned, continued to have challenges. Her life did not unfold problem-free. But Thelma has learned to give thanks. Gratitude ushers in joy. Those who can't or don't feel grateful miss a blessing.

> *"My job is to take care of the possible and trust God with the impossible."*

My friend Fred discovered the blessing of gratitude when he went golfing with a friend. The two strolled the lush course lined with sweetly-scented bushes under a cobalt sky with cotton clouds. Fred's friend said, **"I'm an Atheist. The hard part of not believing in God is that on a gorgeous day like this, I have no one to thank."** It can be deeply satisfying to express gratitude.

An Ivy League study supports the value of worship, belief and expressing thanks. Yale psychologist Daniel Mochon and colleagues at Harvard and Duke universities discovered that people leaving religious services felt slightly happier than those going in — and the more regularly people attended religious services, the happier they felt overall.

If you want to **stay positive**, don't shortchange religious faith.

As my friend Thelma taught me, true believers exude joy. Thelma does. And I love her for it.

RULE #

LEARN TO SAY "NO"

GRACIOUSLY

John's the size of a mountain. His grin looks like a slice of watermelon. He's as funny as an HBO comedy special. I can't tell you exactly how wide his shoulders are—but don't try to get on the elevator with him at exactly the same time. This giant of a fellow also came equipped with a surprisingly tender heart. He's a big man with a big need to be liked.

If you ask John to do you a favor, he'll say, "yes." Even if he's pretty sure he can't do whatever you're asking, he'll still agree to do it. John struggles to say "no" because he likes to be liked. That's ironic because constantly saying "yes" has lost John several friends.

John's job keeps him busy more than 40 hours a week. His pretty, young wife likes attention. When he drives, showers or watches TV, work and family responsibilities dance in his mind. A part-time second job consumes a significant chunk of time. Every morning, John gets up early, dresses, then pulls into a slow river of traffic for an hour's commute each day, each way. John can't physically do everything he's agreed to do. **When John says "yes," he means well. But the people who expect him to do what he promised get disappointed.** Then they proceed to get angry when he doesn't follow through.

John knows the weight of guilt. He doesn't answer his phone without first checking his Caller ID. He avoids people he's promised to help and doesn't return their calls. After awhile, he loses those relationships. **By trying to ensure his friendships, John loses friends. All because he won't say "no."**

If we always say "yes," we sometimes run as great or greater danger of severing relationships than if we gently refuse right off the bat.

We have limits to our time, energy and interests. While we enjoy how it feels to please others, we also know it's important to keep our lives balanced. When we can help, we should. Nobody profits from acting selfishly. But when we stretch too far, we hurt our family, our employer and ourselves by agreeing to give more than we actually can. When we dole out too much, we end up depleted and stressed. Better simply to say "no."

> ## "Learn to say 'no.'
> *It will be of more use to you than to be able to read Latin.*"
>
> — **CHARLES H. SPURGEON,** *Theologian*

But that leaves us with a real problem: How do we say "no" without hurting people's feelings? Obviously whoever asks us to chair the committee, loan the money or help with the move, would like us to say "yes." If we need or want to refuse, how can we do that graciously?

As you turn people down, BUILD THEM UP.

Let's say a friend wants to borrow money, but you don't have enough to lend. One response might be, "Sylvia, I don't have the money to give you. I wish I did. I'm so sorry that you're in a bind right now. Thank you for honoring me by asking me to help you." After she responds, you might ask if it would benefit her if you'd help brainstorm other people she might ask or think of jobs she might snag on short notice to get some quick cash. **Your goal is to get the message across that you're honored** Sylvia asked you and that you care. While you can't help at this point with dollars— you are willing to help in other ways.

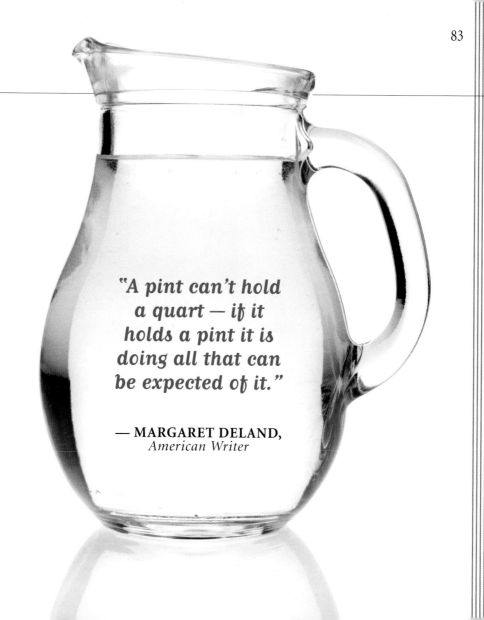

"A pint can't hold a quart — if it holds a pint it is doing all that can be expected of it."

— **MARGARET DELAND,**
American Writer

If Sylvia is a pest (rather than a friend), you can still build her up: **"Sylvia, you've asked me before and the answer is 'no.' When you keep asking, you put me in a spot that makes me feel uncomfortable. I do admire your tenacity. You've always had a lot of spunk."**

If Sylvia says, "Yes, but I need the money…"

Stay friendly, but firm: **"Sylvia, somehow I'm not making this clear—the answer is 'no.'"** If you stay gracious, Sylvia can't legitimately get angry with you. If she chooses to get angry, you need to realize that she is stepping over a legitimate boundary. If Sylvia gets mad and stops calling, you'll have a clear conscience (and no more annoying phone calls.)

If someone asks you to donate your time and money, thank them for the opportunity. Donate if you can, but if you can't give at that particular time, you might say, **"I can't help this year, but I fully support that cause and deeply appreciate the work you are doing. Thank you for asking me to help. Please feel free to ask me again next year."**

If they're any good at telemarketing at all, they'll persist. Stand firm, but be gracious. You can reply, **"No, as I said, thank you for getting involved. I won't be able to help this year."** (Turn them down, but build them up.)

Even if you get a call asking you to give to causes you do not support, you can still say "no" graciously. **"Thank you for asking me to kill baby seals and spread noxious gases. Those are not causes that I support, but thank you for your call."** (If a caller backs those causes, you won't change his or her mind by arguing. Certainly don't say "yes," but say "no" graciously.)

NO!

...but thank you for the opportunity.

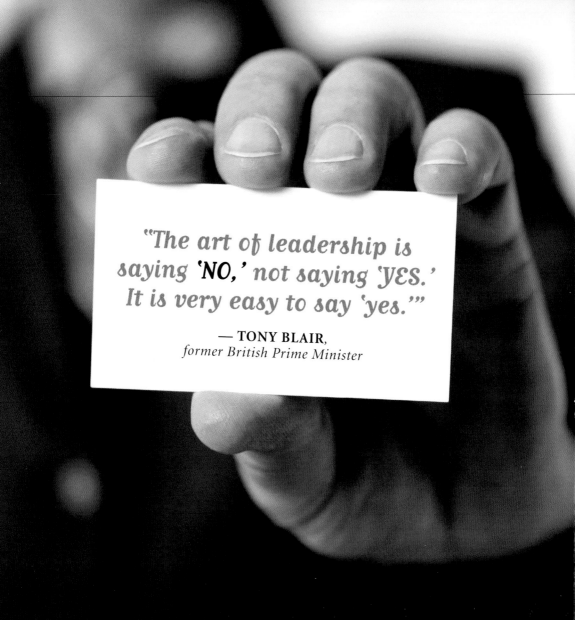

"The art of leadership is saying 'NO,' not saying 'YES.' It is very easy to say 'yes.'"

— TONY BLAIR,
former British Prime Minister

If the caller persists with reasons you should kill baby seals or spoil the environment, don't quarrel. You can even cut off the conversation with a pleasant tone of voice. Use their name if you've heard it: **"John, as I said, I do not support that cause so I do not want to help, but thank you for your call. I am going to hang up now. Good night."** And hang up.

One last note: Don't be wishy-washy. Don't say, "Maybe" or I'll try to make it" if you have no intention of going or doing what's been asked. Instead, say, **"No. I can't make it. But thank you so much for inviting me. It's always fun to be with you."**

Answering "maybe" when you truly mean "no" simply teases the other person and that most often leads to hard feelings.

John still struggles with saying "no." He can't seem to make that sliver of a word come out of his wide mouth. You can.

No one has the right to pressure you. Friends won't.

When you don't have the time, the resources or the interest to say "yes," remember the formula for turning people down graciously:

As you turn people down, build them up.

RULE #
9

I will not wear white after labor day. I will not wear white after labor day.

Understand the POWER *of*
DISCIPLINE

L illy Mae could ignore her teachers and still end up with an enviable report card. Because of her curious mind, she knew a smattering about everything from how the moon affects the tides, to surviving a freezing weekend without a tent in the forest, to cooking a chocolate soufflé, to what headlines covered that day's front page. Lilly inherited both property and money when her father died. She married a handsome military officer in a lavish wedding while on an extended trip to Alaska. She had bright parents, opportunities, a good mind and a solid education.

> "*The good Lord gave you a
> body that can stand most anything.
> It's your mind you have to convince.*"
>
> — **VINCE LOMBARDI**,
> *Long-time Green Bay Packers Coach*

Unfortunately, Lilly's parents never disciplined her. As a child, she never had to make her bed, help with the dishes, do chores, say "please" and "thank you" or obey her gentle mother. An only child, Lilly got away with throwing tantrums and making demands. Because of her resulting lack of self-control, Lilly grew up overweight with poor study habits and equally poor social skills. In time, she divorced her husband and squandered her inheritance. Her friends learned not to trust her because she lacked the discipline to look out for anyone—even herself.

Lilly didn't lack talent. She could sing, play the piano and strum a lively tune on a ukulele. Once while visiting our house, she transformed leftovers from the back of our refrigerator into a feast.

She possessed a sharp mind, but she lacked self-control. She hadn't been disciplined as a child and, as a result, she hadn't learned to incorporate discipline into her life as an adult.

Lilly slowly learned that talent alone doesn't guarantee success. Talent merely gives a person the building blocks to potential success. Discipline stacks the blocks. Because she wouldn't work when things got hard, Lilly wound up at age 40 with no husband, few friends, very little money and limited job prospects. She never learned to make herself pay the price of self-control. She knew she had talent, but she didn't realize until too late that talent without discipline won't take a person far. Talent with discipline races like a thoroughbred.

Novelist Stephen King knew that. King observed,

"Talent is cheaper than table salt. What separates the talented individual from the successful one is a lot of hard work."

"There are no short cuts to any place worth going."

— **BEVERLY SILLS,** *Opera Singer*

People who won't work hard, who don't practice self-discipline, head into a downhill spiral. They neglect to do what they could and should. Not doing what's necessary causes them to feel guilty. Guilt erodes self-confidence. As we lose confidence, we don't work as much. **When we work less, we get fewer results.** As our results diminish, we grow negative. As our attitude sours, our self-confidence shrivels even more. And the cycle goes on and on.

The good news is that the negative cycle can be broken!

Lilly learned she couldn't change her past, but she could take charge of her future. After experiencing pain from that long downward spiral, she started taking control of her life by taking control of herself. Practicing self-discipline made her life better. She began saving money, started showing up on time, kept her house in better shape and started losing weight. In time, her self-esteem began

> *"It is not enough to have great qualities;*
> *We should also have the management of them."*
> — **LA ROCHEFOUCAULD,** *French Author*

to skyrocket. What worked for Lilly Mae will work for you. If you practice self-discipline, you'll learn an important lesson:

IF YOU DISCIPLINE YOURSELF TODAY, YOU'LL ENJOY YOUR LIFE MORE TOMORROW.

National Football League football players know that lesson. NFL players seem to have it made. They enjoy sturdy bodies and terrific salaries. They benefit from youth, good looks, fame and national attention. But those perks come at a price. No matter how tall or quick or strong a player may be or how accurately a person can throw a ball, no one automatically becomes an NFL player. Making an NFL team requires sacrifice and self-control.

Long-time Dallas Cowboy coach Tom Landry taught his players discipline. During Landry's tenure, his teams won two Super Bowl titles, five National Football Conference titles and 13 Division titles. No coach in NFL history can match Landry's teams' 20 play-off victories. Despite having players who would have preferred to skip two-a-days in the Texas heat, Landry produced hard-working winners. Coach Landry once described the job of a leader as "getting someone to do what they don't want to do in order to achieve what they want to achieve." That's the definition of self-discipline!

> *"Hold yourself responsible for a higher standard than anybody else expects of you. Never excuse yourself. Never pity yourself. Be a hard master to yourself—and be lenient to everybody else."*
>
> **— HENRY WARD BEECHER**

Doing what you don't want to do (saying "no" to dessert, getting up early to exercise or read, volunteering for extra projects at work or practicing a talent until it becomes a skill) will help you achieve what you want to achieve.

Many people don't want to practice self-control. They resist self-discipline. They want to do only what they like to do believing that discipline sucks the fun out of life when, in fact, discipline gives us the freedom to enjoy life.

Motivational guru Zig Ziglar understood that when he wrote, *"Many people want to be free to do as they please, but consider this: If you take the train off the tracks, it's free— but it can't go anywhere. Take the steering wheel out of the auto- mobile and it's under the control of no one, but it is useless. The reality is that until the sailor disciplines himself to be obedient to the compass, he will have to stay within sight of shore. However, once he is obedient to that compass, he can go any- where in the world the sailboat will take him. Discipline is the missing ingredient that will make the difference in your life."*

Take control of your life! Discipline yourself today to enjoy life more tomorrow.

"**Self-discipline is a form of freedom.**
*Freedom from laziness and lethargy, freedom from the
expectations and demands of others, freedom from weakness
and fear—and doubt. Self-discipline allows a pitcher to feel
his individuality, his inner strength, his talent. He is master
of, rather than a slave to, his thoughts and emotions.*"

— **H.A. DORFMAN,** *The Mental ABCs of Pitching*

RULE # 10

SURROUND YOURSELF *with*

POSITIVE PEOPLE

E ver worked with a grouch? Nothing is right. They don't like people. They don't like the way things are done. They think they could do things so much better if they were in charge. Grouch, grouch, grouch.

Spent much time around people who just drift through life? They don't set goals, expect others to pick up the slack, just don't care. Avoid them!

> "A lot of people have gone farther than they thought they could because someone else thought they could."
>
> — **ZIG ZIGLAR**, *Motivational Guru*

Find people who will challenge you, believe in you and inspire you to improve. No matter what's going on in your life, another person can help you shoot higher, laugh louder and look forward to tomorrow much more than if you go it alone.

Whether we face a challenge or have something fun to celebrate, our entire attitude changes — no, it's stronger than that — our very lives change when we have positive, loving friends with whom we can share our victories and defeats.

Be thoughtful as you select your friends. Find people who aim high, think positively, genuinely care about you and make you laugh. Do the same for them. When we have mutually caring relationships, we understand what psychiatrist David Viscott meant when he wrote, "To love and be loved is to feel the sun from both sides." Friends make life worthwhile.

"TO LOVE AND BE LOVED IS TO FEEL THE SUN FROM BOTH SIDES." — DAVID VISCOTT

Dave Stone, the pastor of Southeast Christian Church in Louisville, Kentucky, often tells stories about his uncle Greg. Listen to his account of what he learned about friends from his uncle one summer:

"My uncle Greg had cerebral palsy, and he was a quadriplegic. He was an incredible inspiration to me. He was one of those guys who had a golden attitude. He accepted his lot in life and ministered to a whole lot of people in his own way. He was able to get around quite well with an electric wheelchair, but his speech was difficult to understand. A few years ago, he attended a handi-camp week at Country Lake Christian retreat.

> **"Few things in the world are more powerful than a positive push — a smile, a word of optimism and hope, a 'you can do it!' when things are tough."**
>
> **— RICHARD DEVOS**, *Co-Founder of Amway*

One of our church members, John, served as a volunteer that week, and he was assigned to my uncle Greg. That meant that for four solid days, 24 hours a day, he did everything for my uncle Greg. John fed him every bite. He gave him every drink. He slept on a concrete floor on an air mattress beside Uncle Greg's bed. He took him to the bathroom, cleaned him up. John even got some of his friends together and took my uncle Greg out on the lake in a flotation device. He swam for the very first time in his life.

They have this tradition at camp that, on the very last day of camp, they get the servant volunteer up there next to the camper. They talk all about the camper and they recap all the different things that they've done. Then they ask the campers one question:

"What was your favorite thing of the week?" The campers always say the same thing— **SWIMMING.**

The staff was a little concerned for Uncle Greg that they wouldn't be able to understand what he had to say because of his speech. So John got up there, with Uncle Greg in his wheelchair, and he talked all about the different things that Greg had done that week. He said, "We've nicknamed him 'The Fish' because he loves to swim so much."

He said, "Okay, Greg. It's your turn now." Then he turned to Greg and asked, "What was your favorite part of the entire week?"

Everybody could understand my Uncle Greg, when he raised his hand, pointed back at John, and said,

"YOU."

John said, "Oh, there had to be something else. Was it the swimming? Was it the snack time?"

Greg raised his hand up again and simply said, "You."

Want to feel positive? Go be a "John" this week. Make someone say that the best part of their entire week was you.

* Story used by permission from Dave Stone

"Keep away from people who belittle your ambitions. Small people always do that, but the really great make you feel that **you, too, can become great.**"

— **MARK TWAIN,** *American Writer and Humorist*

VICKI HITZGES

("HITS-guess") Funky Name. Great Speaker!

Vicki Hitzges delivers high-voltage, fun presentations with immediately useful content to a wide variety of audiences. Her clients range from Microsoft to New York Life Insurance to Nokia Siemens to Chase Bank to the C.I.A. (Southwest Airlines employees got so charged up, they carried her around the room on their shoulders! Literally!)

Vicki teaches audiences to build relationships, zap stress and conquer change. She speaks from experience. She learned how to relate quickly as a Dallas TV reporter and talk show host. She can deal with the stress of speaking to a crowd of ten or 10,000, and she's conquered lots of changes along the way.

After leaving television, Vicki became a publicist for high profile clients including, at that time, the world's top motivator, Zig Ziglar. Ziglar selected Vicki as one of a handful of speakers he would personally mentor. Within three years, she'd spoken everywhere from New England to New Zealand.

In fact, the first year she was eligible, Vicki received the prestigious Certified Speaking Professional designation. CSP is the highest earned designation awarded by the National Speakers Association and the International Federation for Professional Speakers to recognize proven expertise and experience. Fewer than seven percent of the speakers worldwide hold this title.

Attitude is Everything — 10 Rules for Staying Positive is her first book.

Contact Vicki at **Vicki@VickiHitzges.com**

If you have enjoyed this book we invite you to check out our entire collection of gift books, with free inspirational movies, at www.simpletruths.com. You'll discover it's a great way to inspire friends and family, or to thank your best customers and employees.

For more information, please visit us at:
www.simpletruths.com Or call us toll free...
800-900-3427